DRAKKAR NOIR

JERAMY DODDS

COACH HOUSE BOOKS, TORONTO

first edition

Published with the generous assistance of the Canada Council for the Arts and the Ontario Arts Council. Coach House Books also acknowledges the support of the Government of Canada through the Canada Book Fund and the Government of Ontario through the Ontario Book Publishing Tax Credit.

LIBRARY AND ARCHIVES CANADA CATALOGUING IN PUBLICATION

Dodds, Jeramy, 1974-, author
    Drakkar noir / Jeramy Dodds.

Poems.
Issued in print and electronic formats.
ISBN 978-1-55245-355-1
    I. Title.

PS8607.O396D73 2017   C811'.6   C2017-905076-1

Drakkar Noir is available as an ebook: ISBN 978 1 77056 535 7 (EPUB), ISBN 978 1 77056 536 4 (PDF).

Purchase of the print version of this book entitles you to a free digital copy. To claim your ebook of this title, please email sales@chbooks.com with proof of purchase. (Coach House Books reserves the right to terminate the free digital download offer at any time.)

Sannleikur ef eytt,
sannleikur ef ekki eytt.

for Tawny Andersen

TABLE OF CONTENTMENTS

MAQUETTE FOR A MALL'S SANTA CASTLE

I hate myself as much as the rest of you
should, approaching the veal farm
and feeling peckish. I break out
in handcuffs every time I drink liqueurs.
You must not run with them, wolves
are like scalpels. The chief of all mall cops
is Santa. Santa Claws. When we eat a turkey
we also eat its shadow. Santa's castle
is an orphanage for the aborted. A haven,
where undead progeny cobble toys
for breathing children. To save on hairnets
in his delicatessen, Santa hires only
alopecians from the Appalachians.
Soap-flake snow whiter than a doll's genitals
banks against the buttresses. The parapet
roofs spin in ventilationed wind, powering
the saws in his shop. Halloween pumpkins float
in the moat, the drawbridge lined with majorettes.
Shift too much on his knee and his elvish security
hisses like balloon animals come upon
by blowguns. I don't ask for much.
Above my hammock, the sun-stroked polaroid
of Santa and I role-playing Stockholm Syndrome.
It's the polar opposite of wish. It's all I got.

You've got to get to the country. The fields are empty
as if all farmhands have the clap. The trees have taken
off their fatigues, yet no one's wives rise to shoo
houseplants out for exercise. Toddlers with
twig pistols guard the cisterns, the acne-scarred planets
are light years, soufflé years, away. I've met albino elves
who harvest the guano smokebats leave in my lungs.
I suctioned a Baby On Board sign to the rear
window of a hearse. Clouds suck sun-sheen off the rocks.
I've a mound of creased choir gowns that need irony.
My favourite dog's buried in the yard. She was dead
but she got better. Now I have a Mennonite's fear
of the automobile. A raven puts on his soot and goes
to work the warmth from his algebra. Most guys in these parts
grow a goatee even though it's cattle country. Come on
to the country, there's still seats in the nosebleeds. It's like living
below a dam built during budget cuts, loving a geography this much.
Why must this landscape look like luggage left unattended
in an airport to get our attention? Any resemblance
is purely reciprocal. I have an ex who's on the run in Mexico,
or who has the runs in Mexico, or who is running Mexico,
I don't know, is her hair art or a gas-lamp mishap perhaps?
My dog and I were like two peas in an escape pod.
When cattle rose from those valleys, cankles in frost shackles,
I watched silent films with my eyes shut. My biggest mistake
was wearing white jeans to Rib Fest, but it's for fun
we waxwings set controls for the heart of the sun.
Get thee to the country. I've fletched every sparrow in this war.
When the kill-switch sun kicks on, you can watch
lunar rogues beeline into miles of turnstile trees, trees

spilling birds like a sales force at the brink of Black Monday.
Then sucked in at dusk the way a rainbow sucks back
into an only child. Each tree the scale model of a skyproof roof
giving up its day job. Each tree, a little town like Jonestown.
I've used a mirror to repel myself down the mountain to these trees.
Break one's wrist and you're an arborist. Each night the police chief
sings my alibis as lullabies to his sweet niece.
Come, come tend to me, I tend to disagree with victory.
If there were a book about Long Winter Farm
it would begin, 'A river is always too curious of its end.'

ARUBA

One summer of apocalyptic calypso
and my bacne spells 'sos,'
so I lie on the beach to flag down a plane.
No one came, just the sun laying
on its horn and a blonde bombshell
sunscreening her whole shebang.
Why is there no book about Champagne's
most powerful women? Shark fishermen say,
'Morning, chum,' as I sashay the boardwalk
in flip-flops and into the arms of the tiki bar
regulars. Even the car horns say, 'Aruba.'
The clouds aren't even a thought apart,
and nothing a mirror holds is its own.
Today you're the oldest I've ever been.
You're pretending you're me, Matthew
McConaughey. We're the guy who
jumps a thousand ladies topless
on a Jet Ski, until sadness launders
our face. Until sadness launders our face.
When I act, I never let me in. When I
watch you kicking in the dollhouse
of our dreamhouse, I wheel
the thermostat to the max
in the wax museum of myselfs.

My daughter starts dating a dwarf.
They attend a Bergman retrospective;
she gets home after midnight, every night.
My child is nine; the dwarf is ancient,
but short. I recall my child as an infant,
I could talk to her for hours. I can't quite
remember or quit remembering the dwarf.
He rendered her a pickaxe pendant
from plunder hoarded from past times.
As though a pigeon's leg only likes love
letters, I let myself think what I think
I should. Last night they saw *The Silence*
at a drive-in together. The dwarf
made the *Sun*'s front page. A photo of him
in the back of a squad car tossing
its lasso of cherries around the night.
He was wearing one of my shirts, taken in:
'Time Traveller Caught with Miner,'
they had obviously made a mistake,
'To Be Executed at Dawn.' My child's
voice is like leaves gnawing on light,
'Will you be heading to the beheading?'

Hindbrain's pa saw him
on all fours before Bowbrain,
Hindbrain rearing for Bowbrain,
their jockey shorts side-saddling
a sawhorse. Pa saw them wink
and nod whenever a stallion got hard,
and began tailing them when not
waylaid by gout. Bowbrain's hand laid
on Hindbrain's breastbone, 'We'll look
after each other.' What is after each of us
but a wake of collapsing wonder?
Pa saw Hindbrain taking Bowbrain
whole hog and began to behave
like an Old Testament god. So Pa
sawed a jackass in two for their
Planting Moon costume.

■

Pa hand-bombed its innards out
himself and saw to the sewing, then hung
a switch in the jaw, which once
flicked, made the jackass hee-haw.
But Pa's *coup de grâce* was dousing
the twosie carcass in a randy mare's
pheromones. With his sawed-off
called Persuasion, Pa pistol-whipped
his two Trojans into the costume's gloom.
Bowbrain became the coxswain, while
Pa's heir, Hindbrain, got stuffed in the rear.
Soon as Hindbrain's hands took Bowbrain's
hips, their touch became a corpus callosum,
each other's thoughts thought as one. Hindbrain
and Bowbrain, two sacrificees cum one deity.

■

The entire town was in a throng at Pa's ornate,
wrought-iron gate in wait for the horn to sound
and hooves to pound. Pa, atop his prize stallion,
Sure Thing, gawked as his lead hand led
the neddy, the seams Pa'd sewn seemed
seamless. Pa knew then the Planting Moon
had been the defibrillating, Frankensteinian spark.
The beast of Pa's Bronze Age burden radiated
the crowd with rainbow waves of moonthrow.
All but Pa and Sure Thing were stripped of hate.
Sure Thing's teeth sparked as he bit his bit
for the jenny he wanted to bed. The priest swung
the lynchgate agape and puckered to his horn.
Moonhinny reared and leapt; yet Sure Thing
was fully erect, it was hard to run.

■

Sure Thing's blood-bat ploughed the racecourse
as Moonhinny flashed past, throwing orb-spill
onto the undercarriages of the black Cadillac clouds.
A long wake of glow lapped Pa and Sure Thing fourfold.
On the last pass, Moonhinny threw its hooves
through Sure Thing's sternum. As Pa's brain thawed,
Moonhinny's hide waned, leaving Steven
and Dave waxing atop Pa's breast in Adam's
very nakedness. The last thing Pa saw was Steven
waving the deed to the farm as the entire town
square-danced. Yet the *pièce de résistance* was
Steven's other fist unravelling to show the switch
Pa implanted in their jaw which, once flicked,
gutted Pa with an angelic hee-haw.

REBECCA

My dolphin eats glitter for breakfast.
The jeweller's hammer of her sonar
chirps hunks off the cubic zirconia
of my hard-on for her. My dolphin wolfs
glitter off A-list stars at after-after-parties
bumping till second sunrise. My dolphin
and I used to do MDMA together and pass out
our business cards to the weather.
At the Science Centre kids ask
how close we've come,
hunting down Atlantis together.
My dolphin clicks into
the hydrophone, 'If anything,
we've come apart.' My dolphin eats
glitter to keep her figure but once
ate the forearm off a toddler
who bent in to kiss her.

XCIV

You, who's frozen in   your funhouse-mirror form,
    locked out of your   lookout. You,
who eye-spies me glinting   in the echo chamber
    of an oak-treed glade,   veins lassoing muscles
to bloodstone bone, eyes   the pits of Hollowsure Moor.
    You, whose hip-wings   tuck like an hourglass's
cinch: I spy you, Deputy   Delouse, crossing
    and uncrossing your   hairs. Your thirty-aught-six
with a miracle round   in its powder room.
    My booby-trapped   crystal-meth lab implodes,
swallowing seven of your   constables whole.
    You, who housecalled   on my bedridden niece,
an Ursa Major of bedsores   starscreaming down her
    spine. You, who ransacked   her whole life and laid her
in rest. As your constables   vacuum the woodlands
    with snot-hounds, hurricane   lamps glass-blowing in
the night, I check my good looks   into the lake.
    Its retrograde gears refit   to mimic the roll-by of sky
as I strip my cotton hide aside   and sweep myself beneath
    a bearskin rug, its cranium   hollowed for my helm –
I fall to all fours, berserked,   claw swipes wipe the windpipes
    from every pig that ruts   for the truffle of me. We silver
mirror backs so we can't fall   through: you into me, I into
    you. Until the Deputy and I   head into each other,
for milliseconds a reflection of   one another, I go
    through him and he goes,   'Whoa is me,' as I reach
back for his entire intestinal   tract and that is that.

A: Cop killer.

THE OBLONG VASE

The switch of branches
waving sun-bits in
to skid up walls. It's a wonder
no one has written
before a window.
The glitches of trees, profound copse.
All but one of the window's invites mailed out.
We set the table, leaves in a basket
of fluted reeds, and still no wind
in the eaves. The place the wind sits
between catastrophes is a tree's dream.
A drift of shrubs against the house, mentions
come within howling distance of the oak.
Even the most celebrated of weathers failed
to RSVP. The party for the windows
was sad it wasn't invited to the party
for the windows.

CARPORT

With the jewel-bag jingle of a rain stick,
swans strike their crystal flints
inside fluorescent bulbs. It's righteous
how night and day mother each other.
From the carport, see the slow-song
lawn-pines sway. Each pair
of fluorescent bulbs are just swans
rolled into their cryogenic crypts.
Fluorescents bloom on so passersby
can admire our sweet rides.

As she boarded the bus to write a test
she wanted to fail, my daughter thought
it odd a Saab had crept from its hutch.
Three months after his dad mysteriously
stopped making his lunch, the ginger kid
from a distant cul-de-sac pointed at the Saab's
carport where a lawnchair was upset
beneath a noose and our neighbour's foot
twitched like a tongue for a missing tooth.
We didn't know the swans had thawed.
'And forgiveness,' the ginger loved
to say, 'is not their forté.'

LE MAQUILLAGE DE SAD

I have been exercising
a deceased Shih Tzu daily
like a laugh that sobs
itself to death. 'Does your
Shih Tzu bite?' preschoolers
ask. 'I can't say,' I say.
In the park, nearly nude
selfies hug my Shih Tzu
as their phones flash
off its shellac. I dip it daily
to forefend its decay. My wife
won't exorcise the Shih Tzu,
but confides in it when
I feign REM. I feel like bloody
laundry is being done
in our pool. I wake to catch
the taillight of a fresh cigarette
backing into our hedgework.
We agree the Shih Tzu loves
to watch us fuck from the settee.
Not being able to join in
is nothing compared to regret.
Has there been a day without
a dying? I'm asking for a friend
to restrain me from empathy.
The Shih Tzu, a pillar of our co-op
and a dedicated listener,
barked once. That winter
solstice, everyone was missing out
on the moon. Everyone.

I had screwed the Shih Tzu
to a skateboard and was
towing it to the halfpipe, when
a woman, going on my age,
heeled the dog with its true name.

CARSCADDEN ROAD

You scrawl a grimoire
so she can haul forth
that minstrel of tinsel,
the snow, or throw a loop
of rain where a flame
wants up, or tap a piano's
loose tooth to bust
the wind chime from the horse
that housed it. It's an old house,
inside which insects click.
As ombudsmen ascend to spring
the leaves from their bindings,
you swim your sedan
onto the gravel shoulder.
You've come so far
to be where you are
in the same jar of flame.

WE CAUGHT ONE ONCE

An illness made angels
walk as if their youths were spent
in uniforms of slush. Each Easter
they taste the rotted ambrosia
poached during their hazing.

Angels made Miracle Whip
until the factory folded.
Now they dance in burlap
camisoles at The Palace.
Sunsplats on a skyscraper
spotlight where an angel
crashed. Take it from us,
their guts are precious
in cosmetics.

We caught one once –
it had been so long
at the helm of a clattering
egg-beater, we couldn't
interrogate it
without a bullhorn.
Its shadow got off
and onto unsuspecting objects,
a hermit-crab stain cramming
into our hollow things.
We let it go, but kept
its corrugated shadow
to torture in a tanning bed
set to Mercurian summer.

My daughter has acne quite badly.
They call her pizza face at school.
Even the teachers. Pizza Day is Hell
for her. 'Hell is only accessible by hand
basket,' I say, 'keep your chin up. Maybe
get some sun. Save your allowance
for a pair of Gucci shades.' But Florida
in October is as ugly as people say
my daughter is. There's a new cream
on the market my daughter wants
to make her look pretty. Made from a jar
of phlegm Gandhi kept beside his bed
of nails, cut with the tears of Easter Island
statues. I tell my daughter she is special
in her own special way, and who knows, maybe
I'll get that job at the candle factory, if only
Uncle Arnie would die, and some day that cream
might appear on special. 'Tomorrow is Pizza Day,'
I say, 'It's your own special day.' My daughter
is the kind of daughter who wants to hear niceties
no matter what the reality. 'Dad,' she says, 'I'll take
care of Arnie if you swear you'll take care of me.'

THE MYTH, OF COURSE, IS THAT THERE
WILL BE SOME SURVIVORS

ME

Of quartz I know little. Through towns
with all the charm of exit wounds,
to a clackshawed recital on your Electrolux
in the oak antechamber at Linger Farm.
Remember, if you must machete me,
run it by the whetstone first.

SHE

At dusk I entrust a dustbowl
to the doorjamb. Stooks disband
as the pressure system dovetails.
Poltergeists vie to deliver memos
to crows on gateposts in heraldic pose.
Tailwinds debrief the bowl
through its knothole.

ME

Sandhumps dune to sea, a jar
of salve for the whiplashed backs
of interned beachstones. Sun swanning
as the afterglow leans to its confidante:
'When you leave, a paparazzi of breeze
snaps me falling to my crystal knees.'

HARBOUR PORPOISE

Off what Thornbjörg calls the stern,
or what I refer to as where
you look upon the place you
cannot return, one broke on through.

With little purpose but to tease,
eye our sound ship, or take leave
of the whine our prop
pitches ineptly into the eerie.

Suturing the path to where
it was bound, it hung split seconds
in a realm unsoundable by its sonar.
If only we could enter our dreams thus.

The cruise ship's marriage counsellor
spoke to me in Norwegian, and I
agreed, knowing there was only
so much she could have said

as it took the sun – and unlike
beachstones once you get them
home, kept its sodden hue
going black into sea.

No stranger to hovels, the priest abides
with her crowneck cane. The incense's
exhaust of chipped juniper and sun-fucked
hammocks weds with the darkened crowd. Sure,
we've all bought a lot of lotto tickets, but no one
knows where the mayor gets all those trashbags
of ash. But you, you had the butcher-paper skin
of fishermen who never once made shore.
You only ever felt one way about yourself.
One dark suit and nothing else. The priest bends
into your satin-padded casket and turns down your bed
like a radio. As the procession picks up, dust motes
use sunbeams as trampolines before falling prey
to the cocked cobras of smoke uncoiling off
the Pall Malls in your pallbearers' mouths.
Tradewinds nurse paint off the church
but they just can't quench the jinx.

I made a diorama of your eye exam from scratch
and sniff stickers, the colonel's favourite private
stash of weed for shrubbery. Broccolini hedges
my bets with Realism. Gallery-goers caught a rash
of suicides on their car roofs at the vernissage. Art is Art
Garfunkel's arch-nemesis. Paratroopers falling
on hard times were hired as security forces
us to be safe. If I said I had a vision I was lying
zip-tied in a sea chest. A diorama of what the carpenters saw
in half of the magician's chests: a top hat, a hare, a cape
schooners of stolen organs couldn't round due to a raft
of shootings off the promontory. The cape I used
to get away with. I haven't jerked off since you left
the stove on. A diorama of you in tall boots and bustier
than in reality. My libertarian life coach was drawn
by pointillist horses. You and our optometrist drunk driving
a stake through the heart of our monogamy in his minivan,
me beneath the marquee with the diorama I made
of your eye exam in one hand, the other waving a cake.

Canada, you must sew shut the gaff-pole holes
in the seal pups' heads before the rich can be clothed.
Canada, I know you're not as bad as Germany
once was. I'll never fly Air India with a carton
of geese eggs again. Canada, don't you know
the beaver is a pussy. Canada, I refuse to take
medication for this depression when we could just
talk about it. Canada, I'm the bastard born of a Fille du Roi
and a Coureur de Bois. Canada, je me souviens aussi,
but when will we let Québec out of its oubliette.
I can't be the way you want me to be every time
Clifford Olson dangles some summer-schooler over
Niagara Falls, or scientists have cloned Robert Pickton
to man our missing persons' helplines, or Bernardo and
Homolka have Tupperwared the all-you-can-eat buffet,
or Russell Williams becomes the Colonel of Truth, his flak
jacket packed with panties and IUDs. I can't sail out of a Bell
booth with a six-pack and pecs. Canada, I can't follow your
national food guide to save my life. Canada – where the only
difference between hockey and heroin is that with hockey you
shoot before you score. Canada, when will you take the
kryptonite off Pierre Trudeau's chest. Canada, this is me being
careless in my summer swimwear. Canada, what'll happen to my
Muslim mother's back if her airliner won't step back on the
tarmac. Canada, how can I explain this to the geese. Canada, this
is me in a burkini grinding down Wreck Beach. Canada, your
House of Commons is like watching cats doing it doggy-style.
Canada, no one should hero-worship Wolfe and Montcalm, but
aren't First Nations really just second runners-up, and we the
winners. This is what your Right Wing believes. The crow's feet

off your eyes are traplines for our tears, Canada, I know you sell
their skins to America. America is tearless. Canada, can't you see
she's a lot like us, and we like her, too much sometimes. Canada,
I'd like to tar-sand and feather you for not freeing Robert
Latimer sooner. When will you raise Tommy Douglas from
the dead. You're so sorry all the time, you with all the geological
time in the world and me already rotting. Buffy Sainte-Marie
replaced my wounded knee with raven's sinew and virgin's dew,
but Canada, I'll never outrun you. Canada, this is Terry Fox
putting his wa-wa pedal to the metal. Canada, there is a choir
of residential schoolchildren back-up singing everything I say,
the Dionne quintuplets are kicking a can-can, but it only makes
me want to party more. A mess of counterfeit Canadian Tire
cash on my closet floor. Neil 'chaas' his Caracas as our anthem
pleads, Céline puckers at her kazoo while Joni finger-licks
her banjo's high-tensile pots and pans, Brian sits at his drum kit
and gets on with it, but who knew that Pamela would be such
a shoo-in, pounding her beautiful face on the organ. Canada,
this musical intermission does not mean my hatred is in remission.
What happens in Canada strays from Canada, our over-
the-counter culture. Canada, the Tamil Tigers aren't a softball
team. Canada, inside each Canadian is another Canadian, inside
whom is a Canadian, in which is an alien. Canada, when will your
Indian princess greet me at the lakeshore in her cornhusk crop-
top and ask me down her rabbit's hole. Canada, you're the land
God gave to Cain. Canada, I feel like another weather. Canada,
all my mistakes I make for you. Canada, hold still. Yes, Canada,
this my Réfus Global. What me what war. Keep playing dead,
Afghanada. Afghanada, when I was deployed to my high school
prom, I brought my wood-stocked Kalashnikov along. I am
the bullet that carries the gun on its back. My bloodstream rolls
along like a psalm. Canada, slaughter is the best medicine.

America is still getting a few bugs out of the latest version of
the iRak. What happens in Canada strays from Canada. You
know we wash our cars with drinking water. Canada, did you kill
Frank Cole. Dallaire's not coming back from Rwanda,
it's sinister. Serve and get served, Canada. After what you've done,
no wonder Newfoundland is overfishing for compliments.
Canada, are you that quiet neighbour with a queue of corpses in
the deep freeze. Do you plan to tap that, or is it sovereignty or a
conservative white identity, or your hyper-mediocrity that insists
on keeping the Arctic ours. Canada, I'm the bullet that carries
the gun on its back. Canada, you're not as bad as America is.
No one is, not even North Korea. Canada, this hyperbole
is like ordering a hurricane to hoist a fainted bird to its nest
again. Canada, I feel like another weather. Canada, all my
mistakes I make for you. I keep my fingers as crossed as Laura
Secord's legs that despite being human, Canada, I will be
Optimus Prime of this country. Canada, this is a teleprompted
love song, a ghostwritten Dear John. And despite the bongos
and bagpipes, this is a serene scene, Canada. Like you, I'm too old
to die young. The tabula rasa of your Precambrian Shield's
overwritten with capitalism. There, there, Canada. I'm pulling off
the chloroform gag that is your flag and begging you to part
your swamp reeds for me, the standard-bearer of this jubilee.
Your boreal banners waving to my leave. Canada, ofttimes
the obvious is oblivious to us. Canada, ofttimes no matter
how stunning they are, stars sodomize our eyes.

To cash in the cha-ching
of your winks, I turned
to the creek for currency.
It's hard to swim with a heart
of gold. The creek is breaking up
with us and the paper acres
of winter. You unfurl your water wings.
There is a cancer for everything.
Widowers come off the hills;
their unpasteurized tears
lube the kinks of arthritic gymnasts.
The air treats our lungs like trampolines.
I sought to ask the soliloquy creek
a thing or two. What do you call
a trapezist who doesn't reach for you?
Unrequited love is like asking
a mannequin to help you with all
the loneliness of a glory hole
in Chernobyl. The soul is a perfume
that stepped into the wind. How far
from its statue can a silhouette get
within a mule-kick of lightning?
My soul is looped in the laughtrack
of a perpetual victory lap.
What do you call a chaperone
who's always alone? There was
a brass band around your father's
wrist. The trombones creaking
with osteoporosis, trumpets, thumping
against ganglion cysts. Listening is

the hardest instrument to play. Fuck
the soul and its love of bad art. Still,
the heart wants what wants not the heart.

What is French for 'beneath veneer,'
this title or my marriage? To remember
is to become a card-carrying member
of the past for as long as it takes to re-elect
your mistakes. Don't forget to remember,
dreamboat, change is a painful way to stay
the same. My recalled Renault explodes
past the glass factory. My remedial French class
is full of expats wearing cravats. My mind missed
the casting call for *Total Recall*. John Bobbit
was remembered. Mechanics now know Cannes
is where the undead weekend. Remember *Back
to the Future* when a death drive could repair
your sweet ride? My bit part in *Memento* flopped
on the floor of the editor's abattoir.
My Renault's at the factory being fitted
for a Palme d'Or. What is French for
'I'm getting back to getting back
into you, via Parkour atop ruins,
splashing through dunes,
a rattlesnake skin
my windbreak'?

Her souped Chevy ss roostertails,
blows the drift and T-bones
our chip truck. Everyone cheers;
Danielle's so beautiful she pays
for nothing. Kenneth, who has the face
of Soviet-era electronics, says we couldn't buy
that kind of publicity. His chip truck,
my potatoes. 'Tell you what,' Danielle offers,
'meet me after the Ferris wheel's neons
go down, I'll make it up to you both.'
And make it up she does! She dollies
a frat-house fridge of Labatts into her vast
dairy barn of ancient Czech animatronics,
and we make the rounds together.
Danielle introduces Kenneth
to a milkmaid that's her spitting image
and we leave him in her arms echoing
a one-liner from *Othello*. Miles in, Danielle stops
at a lumberjill to tell me, 'Down the next aisle
there's a fortune teller you just have to meet.'
Her voice, like recanted rain, incants a prophecy
of pissoir hearsay. The gypsy's a replica
of the lumberjill, an homage to the milkmaid,
yet as her motion-detector eyes go wide I feel
tears well up and my insides writhe as the Pogo
from Nora's Snack Shack exacts its revenge.
As I sit and sigh, I see that on the spent spine
of the roll the Fates have scrawled, 'Plan B?'

When The Robolution began,
Troy axed his vacuum, pissed
on his laptop, slammed his fist past
the lips of his VCR, jamming its need
to reread our pasts. 'There's only one
gift horse you should look in the mouth,' Troy
said. I agreed. 'Like an overloaded Ark,
this loadbearing arc will sink,'
was a favourite architectural aphorism
he'd recite to his acolytes ad nauseam.
On Monday I dropped the Fabergé egg,
'Troy, I'm in love with your personal assistant.
Every time she brings me an affidavit to sign,
I lengthen the stem of the J in my name
so my hand draws nearer her abdomen.'
On Wednesday she was pink-slipped. I quit
Thursday, took off to the Sahara,
'Where wind,' Troy cried, 'taps the last
straw into a camel's back to sip.'
I met a woman who did real estate.
That's how I knew I was home.

NOTRE REINE REINCARNATED

With a hat like that she's got to go
head down into the wind so the brim
holds fast to her head. But if our
queen dons a crepe-paper crown,
a zephyr could dethrone our contessa.

Take our liege, cocking her crossbow
to skew a peregrine into flatspin,
then straddling its breast to knock it off
with a jab of her hatpin, while all about
the rawskulled rocks, timber hogs comb
in fleets, like flocks of unfinished hawks.

It must've been hard for her bodyguards
to watch her push her miscarriage
down the boulevard in Jackie Onassis
sunglasses and chandelier-sized earrings,
Daisy Dukes and thigh-high high-heeled boots,
past the knock-kneed trees to the see-through sea.

Offshore a witchdoctor recasts her in obsidian.
Rebarred to the old reign's rubble, she reels
in the wage-slave ships each evening – dipping
her automaton Canadarm into the courtyard
of her crown to abracadabra a lit candelabra.

After a brief period of mourning, it was afternoon.
This mirror is selfie-proof, a machine that dams
our gloom. When machines dream they dream
of stopping. But this bulimic is all hangnails
with a hankering to throat-sing. My body's a template.
My goal weight, zero. I cling to my mirror's
Teflon hug. My body is the lobby of
a mile-long, mid-century motel my mind
must unknock the doors of. Those aren't paparazzi,
they're projectionists looping an old me over
now me, lying on the beach in nothing but a floss-thin throng
of scars. All the pets from my childhood films are dead. Turn me
into the police or into a beast. Just now I made it rain,
singing castrato in the chandelier shop. My mind and body
aren't that into each other. Telling you this is like
a wooden fire escape. Don't put a skylight in
unless you expect someone to come through for you.
After eons of orbiting closer, two dead
cosmonauts embrace but the impact knocks them
asunder. There is not enough space to replace hunger.

COTTAGE COUNTRY

Ten-cane rum and I'm all
sun inside. Children
in shrink-wrap-tight
swimsuits. Cigar boats
burning by. My aluminum's
hoist-high in dry-dock,
tonsilled in the mouth
of the boathouse,
its conked propeller
sidesaddles the stern
like the burnt-out fan
of a disbanded boy band.

I'm one gin from oblivion.
Children, little Pol Pots
divvying up the fun.
They get some and then
some. Rising for a quick
dip, I eye the little shits
wading in the sun-shivved
shallows stomping minnows.

Resurfacing, I face
the strand where the children
now stand like fusiliers
in class-portrait stance,
squeezing schist
in their pinked fists.
As my daughter knots
my blindfold she offers,
'Our allowance doesn't
allow for last requests.'

Not just another pretty face
next to a schoolbus crash, he collects
teacups like a honkytonk collects
stomps. Bellwether in butterfly
bowtie. Nankeen coat, calico stole,
spit-slicked, fine-tooth combover,
monocle. The stork-bit brain heading
the conga line. Pie-eyed piper
still in his casino diaper, faked cancer
to pick up a candy-striper. Gulfed
in a cumulus of crows cherrypicking
mosquitos, ladies' man who shows
to your nuptials solo. Your guests,
bereft of all sound judgment, bludgeon
the dance floor. Bottoms of their feet
weatherbeaten. Drainpipe slacks, tricorn hat,
walks as if an air guitar were strapped to his back.
Hung like a Chihuahua, bring opera binoculars
to bed. The guru who bamboozled you, wears
speed skates on the rope bridge that lets you
love your kids. Goat-gut suspenders,
veal spats, elf-scalp epaulettes. That's him swum over
in a sea of sweat bees, plague doctor codpiece,
starfish spurs, Ben Hur's greeves. That's him
cooing his want of you into the bulrush-like mic
before insisting the guests gorge
on your groom. You retreat deep into your
honeymoon suite and decant the Grand Cru
he gifted you when a crow cherrypicks

a mosquito from your jaw and you jar your goblet,
spilling a rose onto the carpet. Patting it down
on all fours, 'Ouch,' you say, 'thorns.'

KRAAGRAWGEEWAN

Crassflawse inn myne blabbait.
Kraa, well-nite eights myne.
Fawlfor myne tallintip, eet
twock-tock awn wold. Twalk
two myne, Myne Heir.
Eet twock-tock awn wold.
Myne tallin-knockle int wold.
Twalk two myne twonkle, myne
tallin-knockle int wold. Gwok-kraa.
Krumb-dropple, feels myne blabbait
go herd? Too kwat, too krumb myne?
Eye-upfed wit mynde gwits, Kound Heir.
Kraagraw, sea hear myne appley
mawse? Kraa. Graw. Geewan.
Knockle, twock-tock awn wold.
Craughk. Inoutaw gop. Claughk,
youn Fawstereh, youn Mocknee Sloupt.
Grawkle Con, een im kuttuk, kuttuk,
chute awp, yer kilning myne mine.

A tin train of shopping carts crosses a vacant
parking lot. I said I'd keep my daughter off the
streets but the world is ribboned with them.
The iron maiden of my alarm clock tightens its
wingnuts. The past no longer predatory, regur-
gitory. My ceiling's stalactite stucco lowers.
Living in the assassin's castle, I often wonder
who that was in the furniture. O the thrilling
doorbell! A budgie takes to itself in the refrac-
tion, avant-gardists star-order its bleeps, and
you get what the dogs do Sundays. I know the
world is coming to. The future pares everything
down. Watching my daughter board the public
school bus with two goosebump breasts in a
belly top with an iron-on, 'We Shall Overkill.'
The rainscape metastasizes in my knees. The
moose-knuckle disco of the bus driver descend-
ing the switchbacks from the Keep. Riven by
washboard he lets the brakes drum. The dogs
got here by a reed raft that was weak in the
lees. Colours peculiar to various cadences glow,
gash red, steady in the slipknot of sunrise. Doll-
house lightning tips the dogs off to our inebri-
ations. And, desperate for me, the budgie stag-
gers forth. Its clownpout goodbye when we
leave it for a fortnight with the dog. The waft
of red too loud. Sneaker squeaks mean, to dogs'
ears, go for the groin. Groused a good deal,
paying for such a promise is always risky busi-
ness. The oyster guts of my father's cataracts

are like dogs lapping the tears from spilt milk. The ragdoll dog looks me square in the thighs as my father about-faces in New Balances on the parquet floor. Pearly grain of rain undertoe. My father's my daughter's dog's promise. Ten thousand thunders long means, to a dog, god. The window of a dog's soul when its eyes winnow. Prolonged echoes mean, to a dog, he won't take flesh till Sabbath. I made tea and sat at the table to wail. My handgun to protect myself from the small game of this island. The Hall of Cost is ten gazillion dogs long. Sufficient to have stood, though free to fall, dogs don't give princedoms to anyone. Rain-doubled rivers these days get more to tow. A half-eaten apple covered with a black sea of sweat bees, me fingering you on the settee. My index the first firefighter in after the alarm. Imagine a dorm with all its doors wide as a spent advent calendar, and there you have it, love. O the vagaries of this breakdance. Blissless, the dogs hark to the tune of too much tail. Stripped for flogging, you do your doors the disservice of cartwheeling their thresholds. A cock calls men to toil. O the lisp of your hem on the abbey stone hunts piano stools in the ear. Apian drones, shoals of sardines, kingcups of birdsong, the lo-and-beholdings, this isthmus tipped with a dish of sparrow parts. The burst beauty of the enclave that is the mouth-hole of your balaclava. If I am a candle living off its holder, the dogs are building cause for our alarm. A blueberry stain birthmark the sign of Alltimes. Your eyelash insect spines. It's hard to butterfly-net gods as they leap from one effigy to another. Meat is cheap here, at the Million Donkey Hotel. The dogs see in time-lapse, but we lack the patience. To the dogs we are the SWAT team that water-tortured the wallflowers of their revolution. I rehearse in a warehouse clad in egg cartons. To dogs, houseboats on the river are a sign land is leaving. Make up your mind to repay me in kind, they say. Each slick-stone eye bulging. We drank our white wine dry, tiptoed with your heels in hand after a swim in the fountain. Mastiffs bathed in the shade of the porticos. Freckles windsplashed on your fleshpane. The only proof that we have combs is a part in the hair of the dead; so too the dogs have language. In a book penned for the education of a prince a page was missing. And so when he asked me what flower this was, I offered, dog. The dogs do not care for my river friends. Dogs see our inventions can't be undone. Like schooners taking shelter from a marble spill of hail in a rose arbour, so too the dogs believe the planets unsound. Unaccustomed to affinity, so too they believe in the candy-cane jail we call heaven. Easy to see why dogs do not mind if we turn into the wind. The coffin carts pulling up to other doors, then yours. With all the disappoint-ment of a marathoner calling it quits an ash's width from the finish, the dogs knew we'd only make land a short while. High tide rock-bounding near the sunseekers. With libations lay the greyscale ghosts. The battened weatherboard with no sound hole. A bird and its teaspoon of shadow, the blueberry birthmark. I knew my father had died when the ambulance shut its sirens down not a block away. May he be in Egyptian linen, in the subbasement of an iceberg basilica. The sights of his new city unseen. I am dogpaddling in a lawn chair held up by birthday balloons, arms coptering like the crankshaft limbs of oarsmen toward the foreland of Canaan.

I give up all I got trying to give you
what you want when all you really need
is your own self. Too gone for too long,
or I've never actually been here, or can't be
who you think I am, so become the one
you never wanted: the kind of goodbye
where no one leaves but those who are left
feel it real bad. Making love to you was like
sheriffing a town that's already burnt down.
On the bench of my F-150 I slept with an empty
twenty-sixer of whisky and the only woman
near was a ukulele. My dead granddaddy,
with a yet-to-be-lit cigarette, strums his crabapple-
twig thumb: 'Ain't she just the bee's knees
on the windscreen's pleas?' What lurches must
heel to a rabid wonderful. You could take me
or leave me, so you took me and left me.
Keepsakes are our only real estate. Can you not
not be you for me? You know the wonderful go
unavenged. I give the gift that keeps on giving
my self up. I'm the poultry peeled of its downy
bark, hung to cure in a woodshed's dark. I'd never
ask for what ought to be offered. You've got me
where you want me but I ain't all there. I wish
you wished you were here, hunkered head
in hand in the eye of a loop-de-loop of coyotes
who choir: 'Do unto done as have has unto will,
for left is as good as going as far as gone.'

I like it when we shop together. All of us
at the heart of a snakeskin wallet. Grocery-bag ghosts
graze on footfalls. A wallet where we're kept
like photobooth shots. There was a man
who shot other men from hilltops in Afghanistan
to make a wallet of their eyelids. But this Christmas
we'll use credit. If war were really that bad,
would we allow it? My husband was in that man's platoon
and pocketed that eyelid wallet. My husband did time
for the theft, not for shooting a child. Weird, I know,
how snow allows angels to be made in our image.
Plastic-bag pelts on the chainlink fence like the husks
of banshees in butterfly nets. The only time there's wind
is when you try and stop it. 'Afghanistan' is such a beautiful word.
I love shopping for people who want for nothing. I love
shopping with you. My husband was sent home
for Christmas after riddling a girl and her donkey.
Now we're hugging each other beside a makeshift manger.
A mechanical pony waits for our daughter to ask her father
for a quarter; he doesn't have one. He only uses credit.
Ponies have it hard breaking young girls' hearts.

COQUELICOT

Claystars top you off
a handstand to timber
on the beach, lolling like a belle-thug
billy-clubbed. Be it a brake-cut
Corvette or a stunt plane flunking
its pirouette, the orchid of kaboom
casts your jazz hands into silhouettes
on the seawall, shadow puppets
of all the tattoos you've removed
to tranquilize the Sargasso lees. All
the spectres you know you know
bravo, bravo and taunt you for encore.
Your lips to their chore blow the conch
that horns barracudas to ballroom
with the scuba pros.

I went to the door twice,
expecting the devout.
If home is where the heart is,
the homeless are heartless.
Home is where the hardest
doors walk into you. My child
is jumping on our well cover.
I wish I could stop her. I wish
I were dumb enough to know better.
I had good tires on my truck,
kept my hair as if I were about
to be knighted, anything to remain
badminton handsome. No one
who cherishes their face sleeps
on a sequined pillowcase. I knew
what to do and didn't. Algorithms
are also prisons. Years of tossing
slain calves, tractors, and stillborns down,
and nary a splash was heard. I turned
our clawfoot into a basket, outfitted it
with clementines and cutlets, always
the farmer who wouldn't tend to his crop
of wounds. My child began feeding me
the ropes. Her love was bottomless
and I went down until the slack ran out
of luck. I radioed up, 'Take care,'
as if care is not to be given.
I cut the throat of each rope.
If we are mostly water,

then why all this thirst?
Plummeting through months,
I'm calling falling home.

There is a dust, born of pestled shark penis,
that tests your insistence to exist. Standing
in the shop queue, a pinch drives you to draw
your finger-gun and *bang, bang* at everyone.
A pomade, churned while incanting the gaucheries
of debutants newly inducted to an agoraphobic orgy,
is favoured by mustachioed men of the lower basin
region to no end of love. A certain tree turns off
shadows and only exists in the quartz gardens
of a handful of farsighted gynecologists. A comet,
which barnstorms the Earth every millennium,
turns all veneer to real. The words of Egyptian
builders are tended by sandstorm animals.
There is an occult of luck near where I grew up
whose accoutrements harnessed enough bright to throw
the sun's echo an extra hour or so. For every kid
that's cured of cancer, a healthy unicorn explodes, guts
splashing their collectors. There is an entire town
plagued with euphoria. There is a woman who leaves
her well cover off and covers the hole with branches
and leaves to pace herself along her linoleum
until only the stars remain stars.

'Maquette for a Mall's Santa Castle' is for Derek McCormack. 'The Myth, Of Course, Is that There Will Be Some Survivors' is for and after Þórdís Aðalsteinsdóttir. 'Kraagrawgeewan' is a translation of raven speech/song using various kinds of corrupted voice-recognition software and auguries. 'The Physical Impossibility of Living in the Mind of Someone Dead' is in memory of Tara Pitchursky.

I am greatly indebted to *Alberta Views*, *Apogee* Magazine, *ARC Poetry* Magazine, *Branch*, *CV2*, *Event*, *Geist*, Hazlitt, *HoBO* Magazine, *Maisonneuve*, *Matrix*, NewPoetry, *Poetry*, *Riddle Fence*, *Vallum*, *The Walrus*, *Why Poetry Sucks: An Anthology of Humorous Experimental English Canadian Poetry* (Insomniac, 2014), *The Best of Walrus Poetry* (2013), *Best Canadian Poetry in English 2012* and *2014* (Tightrope Books), and *The Coming Envelope 9* (BookThug, 2012), for publishing some of these. Much gratitude to BookThug for the limited-edition broadside of 'Canadæ' and to Odourless Press for the pamphlet of 'Long Winter Farm.'

Thank you to the Berton House, Fundación Valparaíso, Hawthornden Castle, the Canada Council for the Arts, the Ontario Arts Council, the University of Calgary's Distinguished Writers Program (2011–2012) and the University of New Brunswick's writer's residency program (2014–2015), for their support and shelter.

My heart to the Coach House team: Alana Wilcox, Susan Holbrook, Norman Nehmetallah, et al. I am greatly indebted to Matthew Tierney, Jonathan Garfinkel, Danielle Janess, and Rod Moody-Corbett for their mystical advice and friendships. As

A coat like the wing cloak Daedalus designed for his Fall line.
Can-opening the hatch, a black smoke-blouse bellied, turbines
Unwound, axletrees cracked. And Chris soon saw, lo and behold,
once the smoke shrunk, Ryan Gosling and George Clooney pinfolded
To a dial-caked panel sparking and arc-welding their bilging eyes,
Water geysering up gearboxes, antifreeze greasing their thighs.
Then the sump pumps of both Báthorian queens hydraulicked
A last time as the Dopplers chimed. Kerplunking in a palsied fit,
That beast sunk to the pond's underscore. All this due to a verdict

Laid down by our Oracle Oprah: 'The champagne of all
Anti-aging creams comes from the distilled blood of liberal
Democrats relaxed by a pond's dulcet lap.' Only when
Chris finally felt his loss was I found, deep in the fen,
Lying casual-like but for my cummerbund of blood,
My large intestine toilet-papering a nearby shrub.
Under the *woodchuck-woodchuck* of choppers in the sky
He held my corpse, fist-pumping, defying the gods, 'Why
When Charon bid me aboard had I so blindly said, Aye, aye?'

I'd lived best supporting, but in death nailed the lead. It had
Been an especially dangerous scene, but I had had
The guts to lock my stand-in stunt man in a Porta Potty
And, with a little makeup, stood in for myself. A flea
Cast as itself by default acts out its wettest dreams.
Now, a jillion earthworms perch at my casket's seams
And a writhing half-moon of bikini-clad teens scream
While Chris chiselled this on my headstone shellacked in sun-sheen:
'One day, my friends, we all must step out of our machines.'

Typeset in Aragon and Aragon Sans.

Printed at the Coach House on bpNichol Lane in Toronto, Ontario, on Zephyr Antique Laid paper, which was manufactured, acid-free, in Saint-Jérôme, Québec, from second-growth forests. This book was printed with vegetable-based ink on a 1973 Heidelberg KORD offset litho press. Its pages were folded on a Baumfolder, gathered by hand, bound on a Sulby Auto-Minabinda and trimmed on a Polar single-knife cutter.

Edited by Ken Babstock
Designed by Alana Wilcox
Cover artwork by Kate Ray Struthers
Author photo by Lindsay Paxton

Coach House Books
80 bpNichol Lane
Toronto ON M5S 3J4
Canada

416 979 2217
800 367 6360

mail@chbooks.com
www.chbooks.com

Jeramy Dodds grew up in Orono, Ontario. He is the winner of the Bronwen Wallace Memorial Award and the CBC Literary Award for poetry. His first collection of poems, *Crabwise to the Hounds*, was shortlisted for the Griffin Poetry Prize and the Gerald Lampert Award, and won the Trillium Book Award for poetry. His most recent publication is a translation of the *Poetic Edda* from Old Icelandic into English. He lives in Montréal.

always, Brecken Hancock's support and guidance have been invaluable. Thank you to Kate Ray Struthers for her patience and genius and to Ken Babstock for his acute and intelligent meddling. My soul belongs to the Sweetie Babies Club – Linda Besner, Gabe Foreman, Leigh Kotsilidis, and Joshua Trotter. All my love to my parents, John and Janie Dodds.

Octopod garden. Seeing this, Chris cussed a thespian's vow
Of violence: to gut-weave it an entrail wedding train. Then,
Flinging me the keys, Chris cartwheeled into our El Camino's
Bed. As the camera phones panned in arm's-length slo-mo,
I godsped off the dock, transforming our truck into
A half-bred fossil-fuelled warhead, catapulting Chris onto
Those wily albino adders, now madder than method actors
Typecast as whores even the Marquis de Sade couldn't adore.
Chris, pancaking out of his somersault and into a soar,

Drew his Douk-Douk mid-flight, its blade bright as matchstrike.
Second only to the sun as he socked it to the fridge-white
Right throat of that shift-shaped chimera. Twisting his wrist
Till the knife turned to a zipper's tongue in his cinched fist,
Chris carved down, halving half our fiend from gullet to gizzard
Just as our truck struck like a crane-dropped crate in the freightyard
And smithereened. Petroleum flames phoenixed that fiend in a jiff,
Though its alive side S-bent, bullwhipped and gator-clipping my midriff
As I tried to front-crawl away, flicking me inshore as if

I were a ball-jointed doll not-to-scale with its too-tall
Twin-towering maws. As if I'd caused the right one's fall.
Leaving the left alone to wail, Chris swam up its rear
Ramp of tail feathers, shimmying the enflamed throat – near
Retardant in his asbestos overcoat – his Douk-Douk
A pike-diving diamond cleaving that fiend's soot toque,
Flaying its tonsils, gelding its brasswind cannonade-croak
Into a scat-talking castrato. Fire-polling that enflamed throat,
Chris landed on a bulkhead hatch beneath its singed coat,

You may have heard before, two better than one, some say,
But as Christopher Walken and I were walking one day
We got to talking of the pond-giraffes lobbying offshore:
So serene up top, while below their legs scuttled and tore
The pond's subsurface – pack ice hunks with periscopes loosed
From a glacier's lip – until a bleach-blonde with her dog noosed
In its leash screamed and barked as some four-breasted beast
Who burst from the deep and with Gorgon squawks creased
Our pleasant Sunday, like the linen suit I'd slept in for weeks.

That Layer-of-Leda, a Child of Chernobyl, an eyesore.
Throats flailing like unmanned firehoses at full-bore, or
Two tenors in tantrum, beaks braying like Kraken-sired foals
In a canyon of crystal bells where kamikazes collect the tolls.
The mauve purse of each bill begging for bankruptcy
As Walken and I bolted from this garden-gone-Gethsemane;
Flâneurs folded at the knees when Olde Two-Beaks reached as one
And, with fine Siamese formation, deboned that blonde's Dalmatian,
Dolling its dim innards out as alms for a cavernous sun –

Or like auguries the Oracle at Delphi divines at each demi-god's
Birth. Then, swirling its cotton-candy girth, whipsawed
The pond's skin of paddle boaters and bathers like a surgeon
Swipes a dining table for the impromptu caesarean
Of a stillborn unicorn or twin-breached cherubim.
That sawtoothed soothsayer tweezed the gamy limbs
Off a dozen or more picnickers, spurting gushes
Of arterial spray, then replanted the limbs as bulrushes
Or five-fingered crocuses, bejewelling the rim of such-and-such's

THE GARDEN OF DELETE

The world is my cloister and it's belittling
to look a lot like Christmas. Everywhere
I go, I feel like I'm being swallowed.
Come Kingdom Come, I'll play violin
in this sympathy and rub out all the songs
I've heard assassins hum while hiding
in some shrubs nearby. The change
in my pocket is dying to be a cheap
tambourine. Nothing can beat
the way I feel until I don't. It's a disaster,
being songwet and entering silence.
In a luchador mask I sweep up sherds
from the piñata autopsy. The grass is always
greener if you use pesticides. I come in
baring my teeth as gifts. When Silence lands,
the phonograph factory turns to photographs.
A clobber of sunrays bashes in the greenhouse,
eddies against the wolfhound jackknifed
on the floorboards, then guns for the tar dark.

THE PHYSICAL IMPOSSIBILITY OF LIVING
IN THE MIND OF SOMEONE DEAD

How a pheasant in the unpleasant suck
of a tornado lets go of its vowels and sinks
its ditty with glass mallets into the supercell
of cancer that balloons on your pancreas
for which you now take chemo, as though
after the parade had passed I scoffed your half
of the wishbone, pried from a pheasant's
down breast, a pheasant downed by the starspread
of duckshot laid like a balled gown in a hope chest,
its Javexed hem of seafoam flung from the bottom
rung of a dress rabid in pirouettes, a pheasant caught
rearing a decoy as if the real McCoy, it froths
on the rump of that sham then flocks off aloft
to a ceiling fan to cram its beak in breast
bereft with its own incest, a gown you shucked
moments before you drowned as it was weighing
you down, like owning the only telephone and dying
so far from home, that gown balled like a pheasant
cleft from what's left of the seafoam's jest,
a pheasant crowned with a flock of deadlights
as mopeds bring go-go dancers to the unrest,
a gown whiter than a chef's jacket at the start
of her shift from meringue to this mess, a house
on a hill where no one will live due to its love
of asbestos, a gown on a ghostship that ran
aground near the wedding while yours was
at the seamstress getting sequins sewn in its
inseam which seagulls brought in exchange
for whipped cream and a gnaw on your pancreas,

and in my own Baptist way I made this
group of nuns wade into a dead shark's tank
and menstruate all at once, but it wouldn't take
and be undead, 'Too dead,' the janitor said,
pointing his mop head at the exit.

SCAPA FLOW

With no Norse sense
I sat with my feet
in the first fathom
of a broken-down
fjord. Yachts
in scaffolds
at season's end,
the landlocked fish
and chip trucks
boarded up.

On a beach pebbled
with the gallstones
pilgrims came
to pass, the breeze
was brought by
moths beating off
to the lights
of ships passing
a thimble of whale
cries in the quiet
of beating doldrums.